the Handbag Book of Girly Emergencies

the Handbag Book of Girly Emergencies

LAUREL
GLEN

San Diego, California

Laurel Glen Publishing
An imprint of the Advantage Publishers Group
5880 Oberlin Drive, San Diego, CA 92121-4794
www.advantagebooksonline.com

The handbag book of girly emergencies.
     p.cm.
  ISBN 1-57145-881-6
    1. Women--Life skills guides. 2. Women--Conduct of life. 3. Women--Health and hygiene. 4. Man-woman relationships. 5. Beauty, Personal.

  HQ1221 .H24 2002
  646.7'0082--dc21

                             2002071265

Publisher: Allen Orso
Associate Publisher: Rachel Petrella
Project Editor: Victoria Bullman
Production Editor: Mana Monzavi

Printed and bound in Canada by Friesens.

3 4 5 6 7   07 06 05 04 03

First published in the United Kingdom in 2001 by Vermilion,
an imprint of Ebury Press, Random House,
20 Vauxhall Bridge Road, London SW1V 2SA, England.

The author is a white-wine swilling London girly whose social life is all too frequently interrupted by the demands of her job as a journalist. This job and a teenage stint in the army, have equipped her with all sorts of essential survival techniques—not least deflecting full-frontal attacks, poorly executed night exercises and learning how to conceal a hairdryer in her ration pack. Nowadays she is more frequently seen clutching her bag in nightclubs or sneaking her way into freebie parties and then trying to function at work with a hangover.

With special thanks to the wine-swilling women who always get through girly emergencies with style: Anne, Bron, Kate, Lee, Leeanne, Nicola, Paula, and Shona. And with special thanks to Bobbi and Joni for those red-hot sex tips.

Contents

Sometimes we need a little help to *get us through*—especially if we don't have an older sister or experienced friend to help with sticky situations.

In *the Handbag Book of Girly Emergencies* you'll find advice, hints, and tips to *see you through*—including how to be a beach babe, beauty secrets to make you really sparkle, staying out all night in style, and intimate advice on coping with eavesdropping roommates and squeaky beds.

There is some serious stuff here too—mainly on staying healthy—but it is all done in handbag girly style so that you don't have to stop having fun to look and feel good. Enjoy!

Sex and Relationships

We're going to take you on a ride through some of the possible boy dilemmas a girly might face as a single girl or in a relationship. Let's start with how to find a man.

How to survive a blind date

Do

🔸 go with a light-hearted approach.

🔸 have a laugh—make it a double date or a group situation so it won't be so awkward.

🔸 arrange to meet your friends the next day so you can have a laugh if it was bad, boast if he was gorgeous.

Don't

🔸 assume you'll meet the man of your dreams.

🔸 feel you have to see him again if he asks.

🔸 be put off if it was a disaster—try again.

> ### Handy love hint
> The best way to get the attention of someone you fancy? It's simple. Be really friendly when you do see or talk to him, but don't pay him too much attention. Uncertainty is the best aphrodisiac in the world.

On-line dating

There are lots of Internet dating services and some of them are free. Have a peek at some of the ads—it's always a laugh and you might find someone you fancy the sound of. A smart girly never gets lulled into a false sense of security, though. Remember, these are relative strangers.

Help, I feel like I never meet interesting men

Keep your options wide open

Don't miss out on someone gorgeous just because you are always looking for a particular type. Try an older or a younger man for a bit of fun and variety.

Older men are fascinated by younger women because they hanker over what they've lost—a firm, sexy body—and they love the chance to play cool and sophisticated, and splash a bit of cash. For younger men, there's nothing like the allure of a confident, older woman who is experienced in every way—especially sex—and comfortable with her body.

Now you can't assume that all younger men are immature bimbos and that all older men are suave, sophisticated, and mature, but a little bit of stereotyping can be useful. So go on, you could do a lot worse than to try these tips to meet a guy of the age you desire.

How to find a younger man

Think back to all the things you used to do five or so years ago—clubbing, concerts, you name it—and go back and do them all again. Find out what music is hip and, perhaps more crucially, what isn't.

One of the places you can usually rely on to meet people of all ages is work—make friends with the younger girls in the office and take up their invitations to house parties and the pub to check out their friends. As the "older" woman, you'll seem endlessly fascinating and experienced.

Girly brownie points
If you hate his mother or best friend, keep it to yourself—as much as you might want to scream at the very thought of them—and restrict your rantings to moaning with your friends.

Younger man

Pros

- Sexy, firm, fit body
- Fewer hang-ups and fewer bad relationships to be scarred from
- You can enjoy looking at his friends, too...
- Open to instruction from the sexually experienced older woman (that's you, silly!)

Cons

- Sexually inexperienced?
- No money
- Smelly apartment and roommates always hanging around
- Your insecurity about younger women around him

How to find an older man

Our advice is to forget clubs and crazy bars—try some more sophisticated bars and members-only clubs. Bone up on current affairs if you aren't in touch. Accept dinner party invitations from older friends and people at work.

It might sound clichéd, but it works—try galleries, bookshops, cafés, and quieter wine bars. As the younger woman, you'll seem hip, trendy, and full of life.

When you hate your best friend's boyfriend
Don't tell her until she's going out with the next bloke—then get it off your chest.

Older men

Pros

- Sexually experienced—you hope...
- Often richer and more successful
- Because of the above, more likely to have their own home(s), cars, and money to lavish on you
- More confident, self assured—they've been through that twenties angst already
- You're the "nubile young thing"

Cons

- Baggage: ex-wives, weird pasts
- Don't always wear their age well
- Nothing in common with your friends or with you out of bed...

Girly guide to pulling effortlessly

- Spend ages making yourself look gorgeous, but wear your worst undies, and you're bound to get lucky.

- Go out with a friend who really makes you laugh (it helps if you're both the same number on the looks scale).

- Pick a bar that is teeming with gorgeous men, then get your drinks and sit somewhere central and very visible.

- Drink enough to have fun, but don't get too drunk.

- Don't look around the room until you've been there at least half an hour. Joke, laugh, look animated.

- Scan the room, catch a few eyes here and there, and smile fleetingly.

- Go back to talking to your friend, giving off mixed vibes. You're interested in who's there, but you are having fun anyway.

- Look surprised, but pleased, if someone you fancy comes over to talk.

- Sit back, don't try too hard to impress, relax, and enjoy the attention. You've done it!

Help, he hasn't called...

According to dating agencies, fewer than half of first dates will lead to a second date. So here are some tips on how to get him to call:

Don't
- talk about your problems, especially your ex-boyfriend!
- brag about your sexual conquests.
- have sex—wait until you've worked out whether he's worth it or a waste of space.

Do
- be a good listener and be interested in him.
- relax and don't pin all your hopes on it working out.
- look deep into his eyes (practice on your friends first, so you look intrigued rather than crazy).
- avoid getting drunk.

How to date two men at once

The key is business—blame it on work, pressure, and trips away. Let them think you're hardly ever free, and they won't expect you always to be available, leaving you free to see the other guy. This way, lying will be less necessary.

- Let one in on the secret—usually the one who came last. That way you're only really having to lie to one of them. And the one who "knows" will feel you'd really like to be with him, but...
- Be fair. Don't declare undying love to either of them. Use the "I just want to have fun and not get heavy" line.
- Don't tell friends you can't trust with the secret. They'll be so jealous, they'll be dying to blow your cover and tell on you.

How to avoid detection

- Have rock-solid alibis—it's best to choose nonmutual, slightly mysterious "friends" or work contacts.
- Don't make traceable phone calls—especially if you live with your partner—and watch out for the giveaway text message.
- Be careful of e-mails if your boyfriend has access to your computer.
- Don't leave receipts or matchboxes from restaurants in your purse where he can find them.

What to do if you get caught

Want to keep your boyfriend?

🔹 If you want to keep going, tough it out and never, ever admit it. And if you do break down, say it was only the once.

🔹 Say it made you realize how lucky you are to have him—*he* wasn't half as nice or good in bed.

Had enough of double lust?

🔹 If you really are feeling the effects of such a hectic love life, admit it, be suitably apologetic, and let him dump you.

> ### *Super-selfish survival tip*
> Don't stop seeing your friends when you fall in lust—you'll need them to pick up the pieces when it all ends in tears.

How to tell if he is seeing someone else

Look out for the signs listed previously (but less subtle, as he is a bloke).

He probably *is* if:

- he seems nervous if you turn up at his place unannounced.
- he is often busy and doesn't say where he's been.
- he doesn't introduce you to his friends or family.
- he doesn't take you to the places he goes to with the boys.
- he doesn't want sex every time, even though he was always angling for it in the past.
- he has a sudden increase in work commitments or "new" friends.
- he seems more distracted than usual—or just acting out of character generally, even if doing unusually "nice" things.

I always go in headfirst and scare men off!

Overeagerness can put men off. Think about it. If you make a new friend, you don't obsess about her and pursue her relentlessly—ringing her twice a day and suggesting moving in together after only a few months. So treat love relationships in the same way. If you think you've been overeager, compensate by *not* returning his call or standing back slightly. Don't ring him every day or always be available—pace yourself.

I'm unlucky in love…

Some girly rules for not getting hurt:

- Assume nothing—just because he sleeps with you, it doesn't mean he wants to be your boyfriend. He might be playing the field.
- Don't get in too deep, too soon—you're bound to get hurt if you always sleep with a guy after only a date or two, getting intimate before you know him.
- Don't start banging on about commitment after the first couple of months. Need we say more? It's boring.
- Be picky—don't assume every guy you meet is "the one" or you'll set yourself up for disappointment.

Girly morning-after tip
Keep a little packet of mints in your nightstand—great for getting rid of that morning breath. Offer him one, too, before you take up where you left off last night…

Escape scenarios

How to blow off a crap date

Here's the plan:

Take a quick visit to the loo, ring your friend, and fill her in on the situation and get her to call back with an "emergency." If it's really bad—like he is worryingly weird and not just boring you to death—get your friends to drop by "accidentally" where you are and join the two of you. Her job is to drink loads of vodka, pretend to be seriously drunk, and confess a recent upset and the need to be escorted home by you, alone...

Getting caught in the act

If visitors call during the day when you're in bed with a man, don your worst nightgown, grab some tissues, put on some mentholated cream for smelly effect, and pretend you're really ill and need to go back to bed. That'll send them running from the front door.

How to avoid sex politely but firmly…

When it is heading that way, don't muck about, just make your excuses and leave. If you are too wimpy to say you don't fancy him, you can always pretend to be born again and saving yourself for marriage. Failing that, you could look perturbed (calling on your acting skills again) and say "I've never had any cold sores or herpes, but I've got this funny little spot here…" If all else fails, pretend to pass out drunk before he kisses you.

You're about to fulfill his ultimate wish…

Going below the belt, that is, but then you notice that he ain't as sweet smelling as he could be. Unless you want to tell him (only worth it if he is a boyfriend you want to keep), the best thing is to shriek and feign a cramp in your leg, stomp around the room clutching your leg, and make such a fuss that sex is completely forgotten.

Girly apartment-share sex

Sometimes it's hard enough trying to get on with roommates without their also knowing the ins and outs of your entire life. And we mean ins and outs! Unless you want your roommates snorting and sniggering with laughter whenever you have sex because they can hear your bed squeaking, take action now.

First, get on the bed and have a romp—for assessment purposes, of course—and listen for where the squeaking is coming from.

Next, if you have a wooden-framed bed which creaks, sprinkle talcum powder into the joints—get a little paintbrush and really push it into the gaps. If you have a spring mattress bed, put some cooking oil on a paintbrush and paint oil onto the squeaky bits—also works for squeaky doors if you live or stay with your parents and don't want them to hear you coming in at dawn. If this advice fails, get out of bed and carry on doing it on the floor—shagging in bed is boring anyway.

If you really want to look good in bed—fake it

- At bedtime assume the missionary position—the flesh on your stomach will flatten out, hiding your potbelly.
- If your belly is fine but your breasts are small, get on top. They'll look bigger from his view.
- Discover the wonders of discreet, low-level lighting or candles on the floor or around the bed. Much more flattering than stark, megawatt, overhead lighting.

We've just hit the six-month mark—how do we keep the passion going?

We could go on for ages about sex toys, but the simple rule is that sometimes you have to have sex even when you're dead tired. If you'd said no when you were tired when you were first going out, you'd never have had those brilliantly acrobatic, all-night sessions, would you?

Passion boosters:
- Keep on doing it outside the bedroom.
- Avoid that once-at-the-weekend-only shag routine.
- Take the lead, don't make him do it all the time.
- Try new things, don't just stick to trusty favorites.
- Make an effort to go away on romantic weekends à deux so you get to spend extra time in bed.

If your bloke is crap at sex
You don't have to be honest and tell him—too hard! And it opens up too many insecurities. Be more enthusiastic about the stuff he does well to get him to do it more, and gently guide him with the stuff he doesn't do so well.

Ahhh–I've just been dumped

It is possible to emerge smiling from a traumatic dumping—honestly!

- Scream. Get it out of your system. Don't sink into a pit of self-pity. Think positive!

- Don't lock yourself away and bury your head in the sand. Keeping busy helps the healing process. Arrange lots of nights out, and catch up with people you haven't seen because you've been too busy with HIM. Make plans for the future, too. Keeping the broader picture in mind will keep you from feeling so panicked.

- Spend money on your appearance to look better and sexier than you have in ages.

- Do all the stuff you stopped doing because he didn't like doing it. Sweat it all out down at the gym or pamper yourself with beauty treatments.

- Wear those high heels that made you tower over him (like Nicole Kidman after her divorce from Tom Cruise) or that revealing dress that drove him crazy because other blokes were looking at you.

❧ Have fun and remember all those good things about being single. Go out with single friends and allow yourself to ogle men unashamedly and wink whenever you dare.

❧ Get into something new—whether your job, a hobby, home improvements, or going out with new group of friends or colleagues.

How can I dump him without being a bitch?

Much as you're tempted to cut him loose so that you can get onto the next bloke, try to be a little bit caring about it before you shelve him and run off to find someone new:

- Forget personal reasons. Use the old cliché, "It's not you that's the problem, it's me." Blaming yourself will make him feel better and get it over more quickly.
- Make it gentle but keep it short. Try to be as honest as possible without letting him know it's something physical or an emotional problem with him. For example:
  - "You're a great bloke, but I'm not sure it's a long-term thing."
  - "I care about you too much to lead you on."
  - "It just doesn't feel right."
- Don't give him false hopes that you might change your mind—make a clean break and be clear with your message.

I need to make my way out of my relationship, fast!

The easiest way is to say that you have to go to Australia—next week—to sort out a family problem. The only catch is that you'll have to lay low and stay away from your usual haunts for a while.

OR

If you're really feeling desperate and cruel (like a friend of ours), just never take his calls again. It will slowly and painfully sink in.

Lifestyle

The girly guide to a balanced lifestyle

It's great fun partying nonstop, but it can be tiring, too, and we all need time to recover. We're not going to tell you to stop doing naughty things—NO WAY—well, you wouldn't anyway, would you? The girly motto is, "Don't stop, find an antidote." We're not saying give up drinking and spend every hour in the gym. But, for every "bad" thing you do, you then do something "good" to compensate. Then you needn't worry at all. Your conscience will be clear.

Take a one-minute meditation
When you really feel that things are coming down on you—be it work or a tense scene with your man—find a quiet place and make yourself comfortable. Close your eyes and concentrate on breathing in and out. First let your belly expand, as it fills with air, and then watch your chest fill and rise. When you exhale, empty out from the chest first and then the belly. Repeat this until you feel calmer and more focused. It shouldn't take long.

Typical girly excesses	The girly antidote
Lots of booze, partying, and generally living to the max	Eat more liver-boosting foods (see p. 134). Have the odd weekend in—right before your paycheck comes is a good time.
Loads of cigarettes	You need to take a good vitamin C supplement regularly. If you've tried quitting, only to fail, try this method: Look for older women who smoke—zoom in on their mouths—those lines around their lips are puffing lines from drawing on a cigarette. Note also their gray skin—also from the cigarettes. Not a good look, girls.
A new man and night after night of wild sex	You want to be able to keep it up, don't you? So: ❧ make sure you keep taking that multivitamin. ❧ always have a pee after sex to ward off infection.

Typical girly excesses	The girly antidote
Croissants and doughnuts everyday	To curb your cravings, visualize your bottom growing in size every time you eat them. Go for cereal and fruit, a smoothie, or oatmeal instead—at least every other day. Take a good multivitamin.
Crazy clubbing nights	Go out with your dullest friend who can't dance to save her life. You'll be dying to get away for an early night.
Stressed-out at work	Occasionally hang around the copier or water fountain and gossip with everyone who comes by. Or, surf the Internet, but be careful to avoid detection.

I'm having trouble sleeping...

One in three of us is affected by insomnia at some time in our life—due to stress, depression, difficulties at work, relationship troubles, too many stimulants, or eating too late at night.

- Try cutting back on anything containing caffeine, including chocolate, soda, tea, and coffee. Alcohol is a sleep-killer too—unless you've had so many you pass out, though you won't really be getting quality sleep that way.
- Relax mentally and slow down: read, listen to relaxing music, or have a relaxing bath.
- Go to bed at roughly the same time each evening. Your body will get into a routine.
- Try chamomile tea and melatonin pills. Or, try writing down all your worries at least an hour before you go to bed.
- If all else fails, have sex. All those released endorphins will knock you out.

Do-it-yourself, one-minute facial massage

Done regularly, this will boost your circulation and keep your skin bright and glowing.

Using your cleanser on moist skin, massage your face in small circular movements along your jawline from your ear to your chin.

Smooth your fingertips in a large circle up from your chin, past the outer corners of your mouth, along the sides of your nose, and past the inner corners of your eyes to your temples, then back down the sides of your face to your chin.

Work in light circles around your eyes, sweeping over your eyebrows. Then press lightly and evenly with your two middle fingers along your cheekbones to your nose and up to the bridge of your nose.

Help, I'm panicking when I really need to appear cool and confident

If you've got to get through something that's making you nervous, you need help fast. Combat your fears by thinking of a calm and relaxing scene or a time when you felt loved, relaxed, and happy. Breathe deeply and evenly, and repeat over and over "I am calm, I am calm."

I'm going out with someone I really fancy tonight and I am stressing like mad

An hour before you go out burn some lavender oil in an oil burner, put on some super-chill music, lie on the sofa, and visualize yourself acting cool, calm, confident, and having a great time.

Work worries

Job interview/asking for a raise

Preparation is key—you must think carefully about what you might be asked.
Prepare some answers. Preempt any questions by thinking up the solutions and
incorporating them into your argument. If you want a raise, think about why
it is justified and why you're worth it! When you go in, smile, sit comfortably—
not on the edge of the chair—and be enthusiastic. Speak slowly and clearly,
and consider what you say. Be firm but not too demanding. Good luck!

Girly calming tips
> Burn some peppermint oil to help concentration.
> Wear blue to make you feel calmer and more serene.

Help, I can't get up in the morning

I can't face another morning having to drag myself out of bed, barely waking up before I stumble into work. In a perfect world you'd bounce out of bed ready to squeeze fresh juice and do your yoga routine. Sadly, we're not all made that way. But, you can give yourself a kick-start by doing some duvet-stretches when you wake up—sounds obvious but you'll be amazed at how good it makes you feel. After all, how hard can it be to do a bit of stretching when you're still in bed?

While you're still in bed: Screw up your face and say "wow" in a really exaggerated way using all of your facial muscles (be warned that any nearby males will probably think you're talking about them). Stretch your arms above your head, stretching your fingertips as high as they'll go, and give a big yawn.

Dragging yourself up: Now get out of bed and point your toes. Then shake your legs and do just a couple of jumping jacks. Or if you really want to wake up, grab a jump rope and skip for a few minutes, or dance around to the radio—it'll raise your heart rate and give you an energy boost and a healthy glow that will last for hours—not to mention the possibility of burning 300-660 calories an hour, depending on how fast you jump.

Get fresh: Now you're ready for the shower. Grab a handful of sea salt to give yourself a quick, invigorating, wake-up scrub—as gentle or as stimulating as you like. Keep a huge glass of water in your bedroom so that you can start getting in your daily buckets of H_2O while you're getting dressed.

Did you know? Doing some simple stretches every day is thought to help alleviate conditions such as asthma and bronchial, stomach, menstrual, and bowel problems.

If I'm late for work once more, I'll get the sack

If you're really terrible at getting out of bed, try this foolproof method for getting up. Buy three alarm clocks with loud bells. Set one next to your bed for the time you want to get up. Set another at your bedroom door for five minutes later and another outside your door leading to the bathroom. They'll drive you (and whoever you live with) so crazy, you'll be up and out of bed to switch them off before you know it.

Girly Get-up-and-go tip
Another tip to kick-start your system in the morning is a detox drink of lemon juice, olive oil, and hot water. This drink will stimulate the flow of bile, which in turn helps to digest food. Combine:
- a teaspoon of olive oil, the juice of a lemon, top up with boiling water, drink, and feel healthy.

Girly mental health

Got the blues and think you need some help? Don't panic and give yourself a hard time when you are feeling sad, and don't always "run away" by going out and getting drunk. Sometimes you just need to let yourself feel what you feel without trying to shake yourself out of it. Don't deny your feelings, they'll always resurface anyway.

Signs that you may be depressed:
- trouble sleeping
- avoiding your friends
- loss of appetite
- loss of sex drive
- blowing off work
- suddenly being argumentative or listless for no apparent reason

Things that help:
- a brisk walk or any exercise at all
- talking to your friends or a counselor
- seeing your doctor
- keeping a journal, to write down all your worries
- St. John's Wort—an antidepressant herb. Self-help books can also help.

I've only got a tenner and there is still a week to go before payday...

Don't stay home and get depressed or ignore your empty checking account and keep spending on your credit card.

❧ Go to any freebie event you can at work.

❧ Sex is free for girls. Ring your favorite man, tell him that you're naked and you really feel like him, chocolate, and wine in bed, and ask if he can help.

❧ Go man hunting—cruise the supermarket, the video store, wine shops, the street, the park.

❧ You can sit for hours in a café for the price of a coffee—take a book, read the paper, or just watch other people.

❧ Visit friends who keep their fridges well-stocked.

❧ Only go shopping after the shops have closed—peer through the windows and plan what to buy when you get paid.

Beauty

The emergency desk pack...

A must-have for when you're asked out at the last minute and want to look fab
OR
for when you've stayed out all night and don't want the whole office to know...

- sexy undies
- push-me-up and give-me-cleavage bra
- f*#@-me shoes
- condoms
- perfume
- dry shampoo
- eye drops
- toothbrush and toothpaste
- deodorant
- sexy, strappy top
- big hoop earrings or a piece of groovy jewelry

I've just got up, I look a slob, and someone's at the door

You know it's not a pizza delivery man or a Jehovah's Witness but possibly your bloke. With only a minute available, what's a girl to do?

Shout "just a minute," splash your face with cold water, and tip your head upside-down for few seconds to get the blood into your face. Slap on some blush and lipstick, which immediately brightens your face and gives you a flushed sexy look instead of a tired and scruffy one. Spray on perfume. Ta da!

No time for all that? Greasy hair?
Don't panic, simply wrap a towel around your head, put on your best robe, and pretend you were in the shower.

Basic rules for fab skin

- Eat good food and drink plenty of water.
- Regular exercise that gets your blood pumping helps your circulation. This includes sex, girls!
- Get plenty of sleep.
- A simple but daily regime: cleanse, tone, and moisturize.
- Wear sunscreen or cream with UVA protection everyday.
- Give yourself a good scrub! Exfoliate once or twice a week.
- Take vitamins, especially zinc and Vitamin E.
- Give up or cut down on smoking—you know it's not good for you.

The two-minute face

Use tinted moisturizer—forget foundation, as it takes too long. Add a few strokes of bronzer across nose and cheekbones. Apply mascara and lip gloss. Run out the door.

Problems–Seasonal emergencies...

Help, I get oily skin in summer
Lighter, oil-free moisturizers will be better for you, as conditions start to heat up. Use a gentle foaming cleanser to really clean your skin. Once again, UV protection is important, and don't forget lip balm for your lips.

I have an embarrassing sweat problem!
Again, this is something to thank your genes for, but reduce the problem by wearing natural fibers and a good (sports or "active" type) antiperspirant deodorant. Keep a change of clothes handy if it makes you feel more comfortable.

Ouch, I've got a sunburn
If you have an aloe vera plant on hand (also very good for kitchen burns), snap off a leaf and apply it directly to the affected skin. Equally good is the gel you can buy at the store. If neither of these is to be found in your hotel room or wherever you are, add vinegar to your bath instead.

I've sunbathed too much and I have sun damage—what can I do?

If you're a good girl from now on and wear good sun protection and a daily moisturizer containing a sunscreen, your skin is able to repair up to 35% of damage done in the past. Go for a moisturizer with antioxidant vitamins to try to undo the damage.

My skin gets really dry in winter

Keep your skin from drying out and lips from chapping by wearing protective moisturizers. Use a cream cleanser which will be gentle on your skin. Take an essential oil supplement, such as evening primrose oil. Taking a teaspoon of flaxseed oil morning and night will also do the trick.

How do I hide a red nose?

It sounds crazy, but it's true that green-tinted skin concealer tones down rosy areas—red noses and acne—but apply it *under* your normal foundation and powder.

I always get chapped lips in winter

Massage dry lips with petroleum jelly. Leave for a few minutes, then remove gently with a damp washcloth or toothbrush. This will remove those dry, flaky bits. Always carry around lip balm or one of those little tubs of petroleum jelly. Lip gloss tends to dry out lips less than lipstick.

My skin is pale and pasty after the winter months

Use some light face bronzer for a very subtle color. Do it at the weekend, so that you can pretend that there was a freak patch of sunshine wherever you were. If you're unsure, get some advice at a beauty counter.

Puffy eyes and other problems

An angry zit has just popped up on my nose

Hold an ice cube over it for a few seconds. If you have any on hand, apply eye drops for red eyes on a cotton ball—it has the same effect. Apply a medicated concealer—just on the zit itself—and blend around the edge with another cotton ball.

Help, my eyes are puffy

You may laugh, but many top models use hemorrhoid cream to deal with puffy eyes from a bad night's sleep or too much partying. You get a great instant facelift.

Help me get rid of my nicotine-stained fingers

Bleach nicotine stains with a slice of lemon—or brush with a toothbrush and toothpaste. Apply hand cream liberally afterwards. A nail buffer might also help to fade the stains.

My Rampant Red nail polish has turned my toenails yellow

Use lemon juice or white wine vinegar on a cotton ball to bleach discolored nails.

I've got close-set eyes, what can I do?

Use darker eye shadow on the outer not inner eyelids. Use lighter shadow or liner—white is good—on the inner eyelids.

I've had a fake-tan disaster!

Bleach orangey cuticles or elbows or any other problem areas with half a lemon. Then apply moisturizer. Alternatively use a body scrub every ten minutes until you can't bear it anymore. Apply bronzing powder liberally to cover up any lingering stripes, or if you feel confident, fill in any white bits with a little fake tan.

My pores are huge, what can I do?

For an emergency "vodka tonic" pore tightener, put a small amount of vodka on a cotton ball and use it as a toner to tighten pores on the nose and chin. A slice of lemon rubbed over large pores will also tighten them. Try to stop squeezing zits, which makes everything worse.

I've woken up with a wart! (On my finger…)

Prick a Vitamin A oil capsule (from a health food shop or pharmacy), mix with a drop of lemon juice, and dab onto wart.

How can I fix my stained, yellowy teeth?

- Use whitening toothpaste.
- Make regular trips to the dentist for a scrape and polish.
- Avoid black coffee and red wine.
- Use vinegar as a cheap and easy mouthwash. Use half and half with water.
- Avoid coral or brown-based lipsticks—use red or natural pinky shades which tone down yellowness.

Help, I've got scars left by acne

Prick open some Vitamin E oil capsules and apply the oil to scars before bedtime. It really helps skin heal much quicker.

I've got dark shadows under my eyes...

Genetics or lifestyle have a lot to do with this. You can't help the former, but you can deal with the causes by getting plenty of sleep and fresh air, and eating plenty of fiber. There's no guaranteed way to remove them (though there are some very good eye gels and creams on the market, as well as concealers), but try this: Soak a cotton square in very cold water, pat on skin, dry off, then dot concealer on before your foundation. Use a very creamy one on the delicate skin.

I've got stinky breath—how can I freshen up?

If you haven't got any mouthwash handy or you're out and about, chew on some parsley. At home you can boil some mint or try peppermint tea. Chewing on a clove can also do the trick.

I've got a cold sore, how can I stop it from turning into a throbber?

Dip an aspirin in cold water then hold it on the sore for a couple of minutes. Thereafter use a cold sore cream from the pharmacy.

Girly's essential, beauty-store cupboard

The ten things you should always have in the kitchen—even if you don't have the ingredients to make a proper meal:

1   Yogurt—eases sunburns, makes a cheap cleanser and hangover smoothies, and treats yeast infections.

2   Lemons—essential for gin and tonics, detoxing, bleaching stained nails and orange elbows, and highlighting hair in the sun.

3   Honey—a natural, healthy comfort food for adding to tea, for sore throats, or as a cheap face mask.

4   Ibuprofen and aspirin—do we need to spell it out? Also for cold sores and green-hair disasters (see p. 68).

5   Tea bags—for morning-after eye packs, restorative cups of tea, tearful friends at the door, and other moments of trauma.

6   Cucumber—for eyes, face masks, and snacks.

7 Olive oil—for all sorts of bodily needs from bath oil to moisturizer, and as a dressing for your salad.

8 Ice cubes—always have some in your freezer for impromptu parties, puffy eyes, zits, and sexy antics.

9 Baking soda—for smelly shoes, clothes, and the occasional UTI (see p. 126).

10 Chocolate—enough said.

To banish under-eye shadows:

Hold slices of raw potato to dark shadows—potatoes contains potassium, which is quite possibly what you pay for in the expensive eye gels with "vegetable extracts." Also eat lots of potassium-rich foods; bananas are especially good.

Girly guide to looking like a babe on a budget

We could spend huge wads of cash on beautifying products and treatments if we wanted to, but sadly most of us can't afford fifty-dollar pots of face cream or weekly facials at beauty salons.

It's easy to dismiss "homemade" stuff as naff or old-fashioned, but some of the most sought-after products have been developed by mucking around in the kitchen with natural ingredients. These beauty boosts for your face and body are all inexpensive and available from the supermarket.

Face

- Quick cleanser—to cleanse and remove dirt and make-up, apply plain yogurt to your skin and splash off with warm water.

- Skin tonic—warm chamomile tea is an excellent skin toner for dry, sensitive skin; rosewater (from the cake-baking aisle) is a refreshing, fragrant skin toner, and you can pour it into your bath for a fragrant soak.

- A refreshing face mask for oily skin is mashed cucumber—apply, lie back, and relax for ten minutes.

- Keep free samples of moisturizers, foundations, and hair products from magazines or cosmetic counters. Use them for weekend trips or traveling so you don't have to carry heavy bottles with you.

- Make your own cleansing grains by adding a teaspoon of brown sugar to a natural, pure soap. This can be used gently on your face or rubbed onto your body for a scrub.

- Make your own vitamin-enhanced moisturizer by splitting open Vitamin E, D, or A oil capsules and adding them to a cheap moisturizer.

- Mix together a tablespoon of oats and 2 tablespoons of hot water—gently rub onto your skin and then rinse off.

- Facial—apply organic honey to the skin, leave on for one hour, then rinse off with warm water.

* Face mask—boil some whole milk in a pan, let it go cold, skim off the skin that forms, and apply it to your face. When it has dried, rub into your skin, then rinse off. You won't believe how soft and supple your skin will feel.

Do-it-yourself Botox: girly, at-home plastic surgery

It's free and it doesn't involve injecting anything into your face. Botox doesn't get rid of your wrinkles, it just paralyzes the area so that you can't keep frowning, with the effect that the wrinkles become softer and less noticeable. Mimic the effect at home—the moment you get home at night apply some surgical tape between your eyebrows and to your forehead. You'll know when you are frowning, because the tape will rumple and feel tight, and you can stop immediately.

Girly tightwad tip

Make your own tinted moisturizer by adding a few drops of your foundation to a little of your moisturizer and mixing on the back of your hand. Apply to face.

Make-up

- Use a little lipstick on your cheeks if you've run out of blush—or carry it to use for both if you have limited pocket space.

- Make your own medicated concealer by adding a drop of witch hazel or tea-tree oil to your foundation and dabbing it on problem areas and splotches.

- Cut open plastic tubes of moisturizer, cleanser, and make-up when they run dry—you'll eke out a few more applications.

- When your mascara dries up, put it in a glass of hot water to loosen it up.

- If you suddenly run out of eyeliner, dip your eyeliner brush into your mascara or eye shadow—this does the job just as well.

Body

- A generous splash of olive oil in bathwater is a great skin softener.

- If you can't afford professional pampering, grab a handful of sea salt, mix with some olive oil, and rub all over yourself in the shower.

- Throw some grapefruit halves (pulp removed) in your bath for a refreshing and eye-opening soak.

- Sea salt in the bath mimics the beneficial effects of the ocean and makes for an invigorating dip.

- For a cheap, effective body moisturizer, massage yourself with olive oil.

- Use the (clean) avocado pit—after making the facial mask on p. 61—to rub over body.

- Add a few drops of your favorite perfume to some almond oil—or even olive oil—this makes a cheap, luxurious, scented bath.

Eyebrows

It takes ten minutes and costs under a tenner to get a shape and wax done professionally—it's worth every penny and will really give your face a lift.

Help, I've got terrible bags and red eyes…

Keep eye drops in the bathroom cabinet. Keep an eye mask in the fridge, or lie down for ten minutes with cold tea bags over your eyes.

Nails

How can I improve my nails?

❧ Take vitamin D or one of those vitamin supplements specially formulated for nails. Apply moisturizing cream at night.

❧ Need great nails tomorrow? Get some fake nails—they can be as short and discreet or as talon-like as you want.

Top tips for sexy toes and feet

Soak to soften, smooth away rough skin with a pumice stone or special foot scrub, then apply foot cream. Once a week, cover your feet with rich foot cream, and go to bed in socks—not very sexy, but it does the trick and encourages blokes to suck your toes.

Girly toe tips
- Use a normal body scrub on your feet if you haven't got any specially formulated foot scrub.
- In a rush, no time to paint your toenails? Put your shoes on, then only paint the toes that show.

Hair

Grrr...my roommate's used up the shampoo

Another stupid-sounding idea that does actually work. Use some dishwashing liquid instead of shampoo—it's not very different really, and it also removes the buildup caused by repeated use of various hair products.

Help, I've got dull and lifeless hair

For glossy hair, wash it every other day if possible, so that it doesn't end up too dry. Or, try the shine serums that give instant gloss.

Girly cheap and cheerful hair hints:

- Mayonnaise (!) conditioner—slap on after washing, cover with towel or plastic bag, and leave for fifteen minutes.
- Have a hair-pack treat every couple of weeks or so. You can use store-bought ones or hot oil under a towel.
- Wash your hairbrush regularly.
- Split ends—the only real solution is a good haircut.

My skin's all splotchy from hair dye!

If you've just dyed your hair with a store-bought kit at home and ended up with unsightly hair dye stains on your face and scalp, no need to worry. Simply grab some astringent and apply to the affected areas with a cotton ball.

I've run out of conditioner

Sounds crazy, but you can use fabric softener—dilute it with an equal amount of water. You'll probably smell like a country meadow or summer breeze, but your hair will be soft.

My hair has gone green from a dip in the swimming pool

Don't despair. There are two items that a girl might have on hand—aspirin and red wine—that will help.

- Dissolve ten aspirin in a pitcher of warm water. Pour over your hair, keeping on for five minutes. Do the same with the wine.
- Red wine? *Really*. It's like the red zit, green concealer thing—the same principle of one canceling out the other.

Hairdressing disaster

Oh my God, I've just had the worst haircut of my life. It's a disaster, I'll never be able to show my face again!

Don't compound the nightmare by tipping the bitch/bastard—if you are close to tears and can't say how awful it is, just get out of there fast and never, ever go back.

Do go straight to an accessories store. It might be full of preteens giggling over the plastic hair bobbles, but you won't bump into anyone you know and you'll be able to grab an armful of cheap and cheerful hair accessories to hide your disaster. Clips, combs, and ties will all help to hide your nightmare hair.

Do tell everyone you know about your horrible hairdresser to extract the maximum revenge from the situation.

Girly hair tips
➤ A hairdresser to the celebs tells us that if you're short of money, it is better to spend it on a good shampoo than an expensive conditioner.
➤ Want to wear your hair up? It will go up and stay put more easily if it's not freshly washed—dirty is good!

Body

I've got stretch marks, what can I do?

There's not a lot you can do once you've got these—and they're not something only pregnant women get. Try not to get them in the first place by avoiding any rapid weight gain or loss—this can be one of the side-effects of going on a drastic starvation diet—and keep skin moisturized. Stretch marks do fade and the whitish lines can be disguised with tanning cream.

Aargh! The dreaded dimpled cellulite has started to appear on my thighs

Hold tight—don't rush out and buy expensive firming creams. Try our suggestions first—they're cheap and they work!

Skin brushing

Give yourself a dry brush before jumping into the shower—start from the feet and work up towards your heart. We use a soft, dry washcloth, but you can buy a skin brush if you really want. Brush up from lymph glands behind the knees and groin. You will notice a difference after just a few days.

Exercise

Yoga, aerobics, and weight training all work to stimulate a sluggish metabolism. Even brisk walking is better than nothing.

Feast

Yes, that is what we said—feast on fruits, vegetables, and whole grains to get your whole system working like it ought to. Eat at least five servings of fresh fruit and vegetables every day.

Detox

Reduce the caffeine, alcohol, fat, sugar, and salt in our diet—boring, we know—and keep up your intake of water. A bare minimum of eight glasses a day is essential and more will work wonders.

Essential oils

To improve your circulation, make up some massage oil for your problem bits from a base of almond oil and a few drops of these essential oils—geranium, cypress, grapefruit, lemon, and rosemary.

Girly secrets—Do-it-yourself cellulite cream

Add two drops each of rosemary and fennel essential oils to three teaspoons of base oil (e.g., almond). Massage into problem areas every day.

Make-up do's and don'ts

✤ Don't use shimmery powders on features you're not overly fond of, or the imperfection will be highlighted. Use the sparkling make-up on your good features to draw attention away from your not-so-perfect points.

✤ Remember sponges, brushes, and powder puffs harbor germs. Wash them regularly in shampoo, especially those flat sponges you get in compacts. Rinse in shampoo and allow to dry before using.

✤ Dab on a drop of tea-tree oil and use "medicated" concealers that have an active ingredient to treat zits.

✤ Brush your eyelashes lightly with translucent powder before applying mascara—it will make them more luscious.

Tips from the pros

✤ New gel or cream blushes are more youthful and natural-looking than old-fashioned powder blush. Use only on the parts of face which naturally blush—the "apples" of cheeks—so you don't end up with scary, 80s-style cheekbones.

- Use foundation on your eyelids to make eye make-up last longer.

- For a pouty, sophisticated look, just apply a blob of clear lip gloss on the center of your top lip rather than all over.

- If you've got cool skin tones (pale or sallow, rather than rosy or peachy), avoid cool colors such as blue, silver, and green—these emphasize dark, under-eye shadows or redness.

- Line eyes with a white pencil—it makes them look bigger.

- Light blue pencil under the eyes makes whites look brighter.

- Don't go for heavy, dark color on your eyelids unless you've got large eyes. Also, be careful of applying dark color near your nose or you'll look as if your eyes are too close together.

- Always use an eyelash curler, but heat it with your hair dryer first to make it even more efficient.

- Blend foundation outward and downward so the downy hairs on your face do not appear raised up and more noticeable.

Going Out

Countdown to a special event

How to be totally prepared for that big occasion

If you're anything like us, you probably think months in advance about what you'll wear to a wedding or big party but leave the finer details to the last minute. Of course, it seems we never quite get everything, or ourselves, together, and end up having to apply make-up in the car or paint our toenails on the train.

Looking gorgeous is the number one thing to sort out before going out. Whether it's an impromptu drink or a special occasion that you've spent weeks trying to find the right outfit for, here's how to avert last minute emergencies.

Head-to-toe checklist:

- Skin—use an instant pick-me-up face mask or try our emergency fixes on p. 60. Most of the big cosmetics houses now do "instant radiance" creams with minute particles that reflect light off the skin or contain chemicals that get the blood vessels going to promote a healthy glow.

  Applying a bronzer is always a good instant fix, and there are now many powder products for instant glow and shimmer.

- Eyes—a great tip is to use a bit of white cream pencil or liquid liner on the inner corner of the eye to give depth and sparkle to eyes.

- Nails—make sure you do them the night before, so you don't get smudging disasters in the rush of getting ready.

- Body—are you fully prepared for those close encounters? Think muff management, toned body, the right underwear, and sexy, painted toenails.

- If you're having your legs or eyebrows waxed, do it the day before you're going out—you don't want to look like a plucked chicken.

Do
Get your hair done by a known and trusted stylist. If you're getting it cut, do so a week before to allow the style to settle in.

Don't
Try out any new make-up techniques on the big day. If you want to try something new, test it out beforehand.

Party gear

Now to get your clothes in order:

Plan ahead exactly what you are wearing, right down to your underwear and accessories. Don't rely on being able to buy the right shoes or handbag that day. A few days before get everything out and check it. You'll still have time for emergency dry cleaning or repairs.

Buy your undies and thongs one size bigger—they're more comfortable and they'll look better. You'll also avoid the rumply, bulgy effect as he runs his hands down your body.

The do's and don'ts of big undies

DO wear them if you want to scare a man off.
DON'T wear them if you want to look sexy. If you really are a die-hard big-undies girl, try to save them for a night out with the girls.

Disguises

Use diversionary tactics to shift attention away from your less-than-perfect features—if your bottom is on the large side, accentuate your breasts by wearing a push-up bra. If you draw his attention to your cleavage, he won't notice the rest.

A corset will hold your belly in if it's not your best point. It conceals your bulges and most men find them quite sexy.

Bottom—Do you have a visible panty line? Check your rear view. When you sit or bend down in your hipster trousers, does the top half of your thong reveal itself to the people sitting behind you? If so, you need to invest in some hipster thongs.

Top tip for big bottoms
Silk panties look and feel great and will make a larger bottom look better.

Boobs—Are you wearing the right bra? Check for unseemly bulges behind the armpit or spillage over the top of the cups revealed by your tight T-shirt—common signs of a bra that is slightly too small, especially at that time of the month. Check out the new molded "T-shirt" bras, which hide perky nipples, too. Does your bra strap keep showing? If so, you're wearing the wrong size and you need to get yourself properly measured.

Clothing disasters

- Emergency repair:
  If your hem comes down, stick it back up with clear, double-sided tape. It should get you through the rest of the day.

- Monthly mishap:
  Grab a cardigan and tie it around your waist—get home to change as soon as possible.

Static driving you crazy? Skirt riding up because of it?

- Wet your hands, apply a dime sized amount of liquid soap, rub your hands together and then smooth your tights or the inside of your skirt/dress. This eliminates static instantly.

OR

- Lightly spray hair spray up your skirt or inside trouser legs.

How to achieve a flat stomach in three days

The last thing you need when you want to look fab is a potbelly. Here's how to make sure your stomach is as flat as a pancake in three days.

Basically, you need to include certain foods and exclude others—pretty simple, really—make sure you eat foods that will soothe your intestinal tract and therefore reduce any bloating and stomach-sticking-out situations.

Prevent bloating by following these emergency beat-the-bloat rules:

Out

Don't touch any of these if you want a flat belly:

- dairy foods
- fizzy drinks and other things that introduce air into your system—like talking when you eat
- yeasty foods like bread and beer
- sugary foods
- starch and protein foods eaten together
- junk food of any kind
- salt

In

Get into these and you'll have that flat stomach in days:

- salads
- lots of vegetables—but go easy on veggies like brussels sprouts and cabbage
- fish and chicken
- fruit—eaten separately from other food
- oatmeal for soluble fiber
- yogurt
- peppermint oil capsules

Do:

- chew your food properly
- drink lots of water
- If you are really desperate, eat only fruit and vegetables for three days. Don't do this for any longer, unless you think looking like a pole is attractive.
- To reduce water retention and have a flat stomach for your sexy dress, add some watercress to a salad, munch on apples, chew parsley, reduce the salt in your cooking, and drink nettle tea. Not the most appetizing of suggestions, but that's the price of beauty!

Staying out all night essentials

Before you leave, remember to pack:

- Condoms, contraceptive pills, toothbrush, contact lens case, sample sizes of moisturizer and perfume, make-up, deodorant, mints, vitamins—and don't forget that teeny G-string!

The next day:

- Give your skin a good scrub while in the shower. Don't skimp on fragrance, as boozy fumes coming off your skin aren't the least bit appealing.
- When you get to work, keep a low profile. A lack of sleep can sometimes make one overexcitable and prone to talk a lot.

Girly tip

Desperate times call for desperate measures. If you haven't any fresh underwear, flip the ones you're wearing over and wear them sunny-side down. Or, just go without.

I'm worried I'll embarrass myself in a posh restaurant

- Don't be tempted to drink too much if you're nervous. If you keep reaching for your glass, ask for some water and gulp that instead.

- If you're not sure what to do with the food or silverware, follow the others' lead. If they don't know either, have a laugh about it.

- If you have to choose the wine, don't be shy about asking for the waiter's suggestions. When you are offered some to taste, *do* taste it—you'll soon realize if it's corked due to a funny smell and musty taste. They don't offer it to see if you like the wine!

Girly dignity and the demon drink
How to retain your dignity when you're seriously drunk:
- Refuse any offers of line dancing—you won't be able to stay on your feet.
- Don't start smoking cigarettes if you don't usually—you'll look like an obvious beginner and bloody ridiculous, to boot.
- Be extra careful about whom you lurch toward to steady yourself—you might end up having to defend yourself from your rescuer.
- Keep your mouth shut if it's a work function and your boss is nearby.

Hangovers—all there is to know

Even with the best intentions in the world, most of us end up with a hangover after a really good night out—the going-too-far when you know you shouldn't (oh *go on*, one more's not going to make any difference now, anyway) and that morning-after feeling of exhaustion, slight hysteria, and fuzzy mouth. And that's just your essential organs crying out for help, never mind what else you got up to.

Because it's a serious business, we feel we should devote ample space to this aspect of our lives, so put your feet up, pour yourself a drink, and read carefully.

The girly guide to try to avoid—or survive—a hangover

Many of you will know the golden rules, but let's face it, do you obey them? Here is our tried and true guide, in three easy stages:

Stage 1—before and during...

- Follow the old wives' tale of lining your stomach beforehand. Milk is usually the best for this but some even swear by drinking olive oil to prevent alcohol absorption by the stomach—but we agree this doesn't sound too attractive an option, perhaps even more vomit-inducing than a hangover.

- Alternate alcohol with glasses of water—or at least juices or soft drinks if you really hate water.

- If you want to stop drinking but are worried about appearing a wuss, get a mineral water with ice and lemon and pretend it's a gin and tonic.

- Drinks with bubbles (ah, champagne!) are absorbed more quickly, so watch out.

- Nibbling while drinking slows down alcohol absorption.

- Cocktails are good to kick off with because the fruit juices they contain (cranberry, strawberry, orange) help your body to recover from dehydration and vitamin deficiencies, *really*…

- Be careful of sea breezes. When grapefruit juice is combined with alcohol, the toxicity is increased.

Stage 2—after…

When you've stopped spinning around and belting out the chorus to "I Will Survive," remember to take these measures:

- Drink at least two cups of water before hitting the sack.

- Take a globe artichoke herbal supplement. This may sound bizarre but *it* really seems to work. A chemical in these tablets helps the liver break down the alcohol, easing the morning-after symptoms. Take tablets before indulging—as well as afterward—for best results.

- Milk thistle is from the same family as artichokes, so it's also very good for cleansing the liver. Take before you go to bed.

- Sleep. The best hangover cure ever.

Stage 3—help, I've got the hangover from hell!
OK, so you ignored the above, yet again. Have no fear, we've brought together some of our favorite tried and true solutions to help you get through the morning after. Of course, not all hangovers are the same and sometimes things work for us and other times they don't. Keep this list at hand to pick 'n' mix remedies the morning after.

- Water. Keep drinking lots of it. You know you should.

- Take an ibuprofen with a can of soda. What a combo, but it's the only way to ditch that splitting headache and pick you up. Sugary drinks of any kind all help—and health goes out the window during hangover hell.

- Juice. Cranberry juice is very good for the kidneys, and grapefruit juice is recommended for the liver—mix it with the cranberry for a virgin sea breeze.

- Herbal teas. Try to stick to these instead of coffee, which, though seemingly the only thing to kick-start the day, actually makes your dehydration worse. Peppermint tea is great for the stomach and helps the nausea. By adding a bit of honey, you might also ease your headache.

- Greasy breakfast. Yes, never mind all this herbal clap-trap; we all know that sometimes only this can hit the spot. Your body is demanding a large dose of carbohydrates and fat. Bacon, eggs, and toast—what could be better?

Girly guide to hangover beauty

Apply some fake tan to your face before you crash—it takes that pale, ghost-like look away and you'll have a deceptively healthy glow! But, only do so if you can be fully confident that you're not too drunk to apply it carefully. No need to wake up with puffy eyes *and* striped cheeks.

- Healthy breakfast. Try a smoothie (p. 90) or a poached or boiled egg with wheat toast—good comfort food that will help stabilize your blood sugar.

Girly hair of the dog

Bloody Mary. A cliché maybe, but it works, with that pick-me-up that only alcohol can give. In case you don't know, it's basically vodka, tomato juice, Worcester sauce, Tabasco, lemon juice, and seasoning. And the tomato juice provides vitamins!

- Ginger. Ginger soothes the stomach after high alcohol consumption and is very good at reducing those horrible waves of nausea. Try ginger tea or chew on crystallized ginger, which can also curb those sugar cravings.

- Over-the-counter remedies. Acetaminophen and antioxidant supplements are fab. Stock up for the winter party season.

- Tea bags or eye masks. Keep one of those gel-filled eye masks in the fridge at all times—it really does help revitalize you. Tea bags—boiled, then chilled and laid on the eyes—also help to soothe puffy, bloodshot eyes.

- Smoothies. Very good to soothe the stomach, rehydrate, and provide that essential sugar injection. Throw bananas—which contain magnesium (said to be good for a beer hangover!)—milk, yogurt, and any other fruit into a blender. Add honey to sweeten—also good for its cleansing abilities.

- Hot shower. A really powerful hot shower is great, especially if you direct the nozzle to the back of your neck. This will relax your tense muscles and help your headache.

- Aromatherapy bath. Add about five drops of an essential oil to a very warm bath. The wafting fragrances will do wonders. Lavender, juniper, fennel, and ginger oils are all good. Eucalyptus will clear your head and toxins from your body, peppermint revitalizes by stimulating circulation, and sandalwood soothes.

Girly morning-after cocktail
Fling 1 tablespoon honey, then a banana, kiwi fruit, and some pineapple into a blender. Add yogurt, blend, and drink.

Bouncing back from a big night out

- Pamper yourself for the day if your hangover coincides with the weekend. Soak yourself in a warm tub or an aromatherapy bath. Cleanse your face, exfoliate, and body-brush to get that blood flowing.

- Revive with a face mask, now available in handy packets. Full of zingy, refreshing, and soothing ingredients to wake your skin up and get blood to the outer layers again. Try making your own (p. 60-61).

- Exercise to sweat out all those toxins! A brisk stroll to work really does help by getting more oxygen into the blood, which then flows more quickly to the liver and speeds up the rescue operation.

- Sex. There's nothing better than a horizontal morning workout to brighten your morning, get your blood pumping, and rid you of hangover symptoms.

Literary morning-after wisdom
As Kingsley Amis famously wrote in his book, *On Drink*: "There's no better cure than making love to your partner the following morning."

- Comfort dress. Slip into something both slinky, soft, and comforting. Avoid red and black, as they can be a bit harsh against a pale, washed-out complexion.

- Face rescue. Try our homemade remedies for red eyes, puffy eyes, and dark shadows (see pp. 53 and 57), or try an instant pick-me-up face mask (p. 60). We swear by keeping an eye mask in the fridge and using one of those instant radiance products.

- Make-up. Use tinted moisturizer to give you some color. Don't try anything too fussy—a bad attack of the shakes and a tube of liquid eyeliner will become your enemy. Keep things simple.

- Do something to make yourself feel better—spend some money or have a nice lunch with a friend to dissect the night before.

- Appropriate behavior. Be on your guard when in the fragile, vulnerable state that is a hangover. You can say the wrong things, forget stuff, press the wrong button when sending an e-mail, or call your lover by the wrong name. All of which can compound your hangover hell.

Sexy, healthy girly stuff

Men love them, but stockings aren't just for getting men in the mood:

- They're not only sexy, they're economical: Buy two pairs of the same stockings. If you get a run in one leg, just throw it away and keep on using the other three legs.

- They can help prevent infection, as they breathe better than tights.

- An oldie but goodie—use clear nail polish to stop runs.

Staying In

I've got people coming for dinner in thirty minutes and the place is a mess

You've finally gotten rid of your roommates, but now you need help!

- Spray furniture polish near the front door. The heady aroma creates the illusion that you've spent all day with your sleeves rolled up. Empty all visible trash. Do something creative with your throw cushions—like plump them up!

- Open a can of cola—have a slurp and pour the rest down the toilet to dissolve yucky stains. Flush just before guests arrive. Check your bathroom for embarrassing objects left around.

- Get a box and clear away all unnecessary stuff from surfaces—hide it in a closet. But, be sure leave out the odd cooking gadget for effect.

- Fill the sink and throw in the dirty dishes. Or, if you really don't have time, put them in a bag and hide it in the cupboard.

- Remember to remove any clothes drying on radiators or undies wedged under the sofa.

- Set the table—it diverts attention from everything else. Put out napkins, candles, and wine glasses.

- Last but not least, hide a multitude of sins by turning off all the lights and lighting scented candles.

When they arrive

Give them a drink and some munchies immediately, and make them comfortable in the tidiest part of your home. Pour yourself a drink and relax—the worst is over.

Girly homemade tricks

- To cunningly deceive, transform your premade dips into the "homemade" variety by scraping them into bowls and sprinkling chopped, fresh herbs over the top—try parsley or chives.

- Transform store-bought desserts into ones that look as if you've made them yourself. If, for example, you've bought a chocolate torte, bash it about a bit so it appears less perfect and dust with cocoa powder or powdered sugar so the plate is also sprinkled. Add fresh strawberries and smear chocolate about your person.

Girly tips for appearing to be the perfect hostess

You don't want to waste precious time cooking when you could be making yourself gorgeous or drinking and flirting with your guests. Here's how to cheat your way to culinary success:

- Always have enough booze. Start with a nice bottle of wine when they arrive and will notice it more, then move on to the cheaper stuff. Finally, trot out the very cheap stuff when everyone's too blitzed to notice.

- Having a premixed pitcher of a cocktail is often a good way to kick things off and prevents the panic of trying to make lots of different drinks at once—and small details, such as using lemon in your vodka and tonic, makes it look like you've put forth some effort.

- Always have plenty of nibbles for your guests to eat while you're busy preparing the meal. If something happens to the main course, they won't be too hungry.

- Don't go for the most popular local deli dishes—your canny, premade-meal-consuming friends will recognize them straight away. Try exotic dishes or buy "home-cooked" pasta dishes and sauces.

- Have a quick look at the ingredients on the packets so you know how to bluff when asked "what's in this?"

Girly punch

A killer punch made from a cheap bottle of vodka, fruit juice, and lemonade, along with small chunks of fruit and ice cubes, is a good way to start things off with a bang without spending too much cash.

- Get some fresh herbs, chop, and sprinkle over food after you've plated up—this makes even premade meals look homemade.

- Don't go for anything too complicated or untested. Stick to simple things—with good fresh ingredients—rather than trying to re-create what you had at a restaurant last week.

Top girly trouble-avoiding tips

Help, I've just put a huge scratch in someone's coffee table…

- Find a brown crayon, melt a little with a cigarette lighter, and rub it into the scratch. If you can't find a crayon, try a little bit of shoe polish (the right color). It should disguise the mark so you won't have to own up.
- If you scorch your clothing, try soaking it overnight in some whole milk. We don't know why the enzymes in the milk help, but they do.

Baking soda is a girly essential

- Dissolve in a little water and apply to skin to ease bee stings.
- Add a bit to your washing machine to take any odor out of your laundry—great for laundry that has been left in the machine for days.
- Dissolve a pinch in water and drink to make your pee more alkaline and stop the burning if you have a UTI.
- Sprinkle a little in your boyfriend's or your own sneakers overnight to absorb stinkiness.

I've had a crazy time lately—too much booze and too many late nights…

You can rejuvenate yourself in a weekend by staying in and:

- switching off the phone.
- wearing your comfiest slouching-around clothes.
- drinking loads of water to flush out the toxins.
- catching up on sleep.
- leaving off your make-up, putting on a face mask, and pampering yourself with essential oil baths.
- detoxing by laying off the booze and cigarettes—you can do it for a weekend.
- eating lots of fruit and veggies.
- going for a gentle walk in the park to get some fresh air.

I just dashed to the corner store in my worst sweats with dirty hair and bumped into the man I adore

Don't worry about it—just make sure it never happens again!

- First, take steps to ensure you'll bump into him again, this time looking like the ultimate sex goddess.
- Second, go through your casual clothes and chuck out any frumpy clothes that make you look like a bag lady.
- Next time you buy slobbing-out clothes, make sure they look good, too. Even sweats can be flattering if you get the right sort.
- Wear a strappy tank top with your sweats. If your breasts are firm, go without a bra—you'll be more comfy and look really sexy.
- If you must do oversized, make it a cardi over a top that shows off your shape. Unzip if you spot anyone you want to impress.

Playing
Away

Girly guide to vacation fun

Despite being bombarded with beach-body diet plans in every glossy magazine from the beginning of spring, most of us never quite get around to that vacation diet, those extra gym sessions, or that all-over fake tan. So whether you've got a week to go, or perhaps only a day, we offer the essential girly guide to whipping that body into the best possible shape in a very short bit of time—to get you looking like a natural-born beach babe every minute of your vacation.

Counting down to vacation...

If you've got only a week or two to go before you squeeze into that teeny bikini, don't worry, there's still sufficient time to make a difference. Rather than go on a starvation diet that will leave you weak and vulnerable at a time when you need to be shoring up your body's defenses, cut down on portion sizes and "bad" foods. Forget the cakes, cookies, fries, and late-night take-outs. Up the salads and fresh fruits and vegetables. Try to cut back on your alcohol intake— and step up the gym visits if you can. Even a few daily sit-ups will help. Body-brushing your thighs and buttocks in the shower every morning for a week will definitely enhance their appearance.

24-hour bikini emergency

Whether you're lucky enough to have your new man whisk you away to Greece for a surprise weekend or you just haven't got around to organizing yourself, and you've now only got a day before you get on that flight, here's a quick girly guide to covering all bases.

Check...

- Have you faked it? Tanned, wobbly bits look a lot better than white ones, never mind how horrific it is to be the whitest person on the beach.
- Have you defuzzed? Sort out that bikini line...
- Are your feet an embarrassment (see p. 66)?
- Worried about that convex stomach (see p. 81)?

Girly embarrassment-dodging tip

Water-test your bikini in the shower—it may be see-through when wet. It might be best to avoid flimsy white bikinis for this reason...unless of course you go for the full Brazilian bikini wax.

Fake tanning disasters to avoid

There are now many different types of fake tan—creams, gels, mousses, sprays, and even moist wipes. The tinted variety is often better, so you can see where you've applied it—plus, it gives you instant color. There are also different types especially suited for the face, which may have extra moisturizer and be noncomedogenic. Check whether they contain an SPF of at least 15—essential if you're going to be out in the (real) sun. Match to your skin tone—they come in light, medium, and dark shades.

Girly tanning tips:

- Mix with moisturizer for problem areas where skin is drier or creased—ankles, backs of knees, toes, and between fingers. Watch out for inner arms.
- Don't apply it immediately after a shower or it won't absorb properly. If you've got extra time, apply a second layer to intensify the color.
- A common mistake is actually applying too little, so be confident if you've done the right prep of exfoliating and moisturizing.
- Be careful of letting it dry before you don light-colored clothing—wash your hands, especially your cuticles, which absorb color.
- Take fake tan with you on holiday to top up before you get a genuine bronzed look. Decant into a travel-size, and thus unidentifiable, container.

Girly beach body tips

- Flat stomach—avoid salty foods, caffeine, and alcohol, all of which cause water retention. (See pp. 81–82 for more tips.)

- Hair—try to have a trim before you go to lose all the split ends. Protect by covering up with a scarf or hat or with special sprays (or even suntan lotion in an emergency). Make sure you're extra careful if you've got bleached hair.

- Bikini line—go for warm-wax, roll-on types, or cream hair removers if you haven't had time to go for a professional job. Try to do a day before you go so follicles can calm down—and definitely go before you self-tan.

- Speedy pedicure—if you have time on your side, then a pedicurist can give your toes a good going-over, but otherwise try the bare minimum: clip nails, tidy cuticles, get rid of lumps of hard skin, and soak or slather in rich oil or moisturizer. Then, after letting this soak in, apply a coat of clear nail polish for a natural look or a bright color if you want to draw attention to your toes. Your feet will look instantly better.

Desperate beach tip
No time for waxing, fake tan, or dieting? Bury yourself in the sand or buy a king-size sarong.

Hot tips for looking like a beach babe, not a beached whale, in your bikini

* Go for a size up rather than one that will be biting into you and revealing slight bulges on your back or buttocks.

* Make sure you try bending down, sitting, and stretching when you try one on or you may be in for a big shock on the beach. This even applies to you skinny girls.

* That push-up number may be great in a changing room, but once it's wet and you bend down to adjust your towel—oops!—your boobs have brimmed over and nearly fallen out completely.

* You don't have to stick to "slimming black"—bright colors can flatter just as much, and patterns like polka dots keep the eye moving around and away from your figure.

* Go for bright, fun, and stylish accessories such as a bandanna, trendy earrings, big shades, or girly flip-flops to make you feel good and look cool. Think curvy, glamorous, film-star look.

Girly vacation-essentials kit

- Aloe vera gel is wonderfully soothing for sunburned skin, bites, or stings—available from pharmacists.

- Essential oils—citronella, lavender, and tea-tree oils deter insects.

- Multivitamin tablets—to boost your immune system.

- Antidiarrhea medicine.

- Cranberry extract tablets. All that extra sex and dehydration can cause a UTI.

- Emergency first-aid kit. Pack separately from toiletries in case of spillage. Remember to pack this or any medicines in carry-on luggage.

- If you are traveling with a companion, pack half your stuff in each case—if one goes astray, you at least have some clothes to wear, rather than trying to fit into your best friend's size 4 bikini.

- Take a long-sleeved shirt or top to cover up if you get burned—or to protect from mosquito bites in the evenings.

How to survive a long-haul flight and look fabulous

Your carry-on girly kit should include:

- petroleum jelly—to keep your lips moist
- rosewater—mist your face regularly to keep your skin from dehydrating
- lavender oil—dab on yourself, the pillow...
- moisturizer—reapply regularly
- mints—for fresh breath
- hair ties
- herbal sleeping pills—if the flight is long enough to sleep
- panty liners—to keep you fresh

Desperate for a flat stomach?

Hold stomach in for as long as you can. Keep your shoulders back, head up, and lie on your back, propped up on your elbows. Hold this position until it's time for lunch, and eat like a horse—everyone's seen your gorgeous flat belly by now. Wear your sarong after lunch.

- magazines, books, portable radio with headphones
- a bottle of water—you can never get enough from the cabin crew
- inflatable pillow
- eye mask
- earplugs

Dress in comfortable layers. Tight trousers can be hell. Wear comfortable shoes, as your feet will swell. A pashmina can double as a blanket or pillow.

Girly jet-lag tip
Siberian ginseng will increase your body's ability to fight fatigue. Take everyday for a week before your flight to try to combat the worst symptoms of jet lag.

I'm scared of DVT (deep vein thrombosis)

DVT is now known to be a much more serious risk to long-haul travelers than previously realized. Women on the pill are especially at risk, but also those who have had recent surgery or illness or a history of blood-clotting problems.

Tips:

- Keep moving around in your seat. Stretch your legs and toes.

- Move out of your seat as much as possible—aisle seats are better for this.

- Drink plenty of water and stay away from alcohol and caffeine.

- Take an aspirin or an herbal pain remedy. This can be taken in the week or so leading up to the flight as preparation.

- Buy and wear support tights, as they encourage good blood circulation. You can even buy special compression socks if you don't want to wear tights.

Girly eye protection
If you get sore eyes, spray rosewater on cotton pads and lay them on your eyes. It's best to wear glasses instead of contact lenses, which will only encourage dryness. You can always put your contacts back in just before you land.

Make yourself beautiful while on the beach

❧ Emulate Madonna. Do some stretching exercises or yoga. Best to do when your boyfriend is snoozing after lunch, otherwise his derisive hoots of laughter will have the whole beach watching.

❧ Don't worry that you look like a complete prat—nobody knows you. If you really don't want to be seen, do some water aerobics in the ocean—submerged running on the spot will tone up your legs.

❧ Use the sand to exfoliate yourself. Rub it all over.

❧ Rub that suntan lotion into your toenails and fingernails. Your cuticles will be conditioning and nails growing faster while you lie there tanning. At the end of two weeks, you'll have much better-looking nails.

❧ Bored of reading or just lying in the sun? Give yourself a quick manicure—it'll save time later when you're getting ready to go out.

> **Girly looking-hot survival tip**
> Take two bikinis—one for when the other is drying off. Also, if you only had one and you lost it, you might have to spend the rest of the week wearing an ill-fitting one from the local shops. Better to plan ahead.

How to look like a sun-kissed beach babe in five minutes

After a day on the beach, jump in the shower, slather yourself in luxuriously-fragranced shower gel, and douse your hair with a good deep conditioner. After the shower, slap on some body lotion, spray your limbs with one of those light, oily, sheeny sprays, before slipping on that strappy dress and a pair of sandals. Put on a bit of lip gloss, mascara, and light bronzing powder, and you're off!

How to survive a full-on clubbing destination

If you're off somewhere like Cancun or Ft. Lauderdale or Mazatlan, try to pace yourself on the alcohol front. Hot temps will make dehydration worse, so don't go to sleep on the beach after a big night unless you're in the shade—it'll take you days to recover from the headache when you wake up.

* Eat regularly, even if not proper sit-down meals.

* Drink lots of water. If you don't find this easy, remember watermelon is mostly water, so nibble on chunks. It is also great for the immune system.

* Try to give your body—especially your liver—a night off at least once or twice. You'll be less likely to get run down.

* Don't mix alcohol and drugs.

* Don't overdo the sun. Use sunscreen with a high enough protection factor. Go down gradually. Remember it washes off in water, so it needs to be reapplied every hour or so.

* Avoid stomach upset by drinking bottled water and watching what you eat—remember ice cubes are often made from tap water. Make sure you always have some bottled water in your room—especially if you've been drinking.

Sex on the beach

Girly guide to vacation sex

🦋 If you're on the pill, remember to take enough supplies to last you the whole trip—bring an extra pack, in case your handbag is lost or stolen.

🦋 Remember you may want to run on packs to avoid having to deal with your period. Check the instructions or with your doctor about how and if you can do this correctly with your particular type of pill.

🦋 It's not pure chance that too many of us get pregnant on vacation. It's not just the extra bonking, but also that it's easy to forget that stomach upsets or sickness mean that you won't have digested your pill properly. Take condoms to use for the next few days to be extra sure of being safe.

🦋 Take condoms—even if you are on the pill—to protect against STDs. It's easier—and probably cheaper—to buy them at home first, as in some countries they can be hard to find or of poor quality. Keeping a couple in your pocket or purse doesn't mean you're a slut—just a prepared girly. It could mean the difference between having a vacation romance and not having one.

Beware of spiked drinks

We've all read about Rohypnol—aka the "date rape drug"—and while it is still generally quite rare, it's wise to be on your guard on a night out, especially in unfamiliar surroundings. It's better if you see the bartender serve your drink, so beware of drinks bought by strangers from the bar or leaving your drink unattended. Only accept drinks from people you trust. If you think your drink tastes a bit odd or you begin to feel strangely drunk, stop drinking and remove yourself from the situation, with a friend if possible.

Lazy Girly tip
To "iron" your clothes while you're on holiday, hang them up the night before you want to wear them and splash, flick, or spray water onto the creases. The weight of the water makes most wrinkles fall out by the next day.

Girly guide to common-sense safety for girls traveling alone abroad

- Make sure you stay on a street that has bars and late-night shops where there are plenty of people around. It's wise not to walk home alone to your hotel after dark—but be careful about letting that handsome stranger accompany you. Be wary of people overhearing your room number if you collect your key from the reception desk.

- Watch out for pickpockets. Be especially careful in crowded places or on the subway. If you're jostled or distracted by someone, it's often a decoy. Make sure the type of bag you use is secure—ones with open tops can easily be "dipped."

- Don't carry huge amounts of cash around or carry all your ATM and credit cards together. Hide in separate places in your luggage.

- Keep the phone number for your ATM and credit cards at hand—not in the handbag!—so you can cancel them immediately if they get stolen. Might be useful to keep copies of the numbers somewhere else in your luggage.

- Get insurance. This is not just for thefts of valuables, but also for delays of luggage and health problems. Check the small print for the extent of coverage—and make sure you get a police incident report/crime number if you are robbed or the policy won't be valid. Take the insurance company help-line number with you.

- Find out the country's number for emergency police. Put it in your cell phone speed-dial just in case.

- Lost your passport? Find out where the nearest U.S. embassy is. They can also arrange medical attention or help in case of assault.

Girly vacation tips

- Money—don't carry large amounts on you and divide up what you have in different suitcases, in case of theft or pickpocketing.
- Take extra contact lenses, prescription glasses, and essential medication.

Health

Eating to avoid health emergencies

Sometimes you get to the end of a week and realize all you've eaten since the last weekend is junk food. Life is so hectic, and it's easy to forget to eat properly. This checklist will help you to stay on track by reminding you what you should be eating to stay healthy. Make a list and stick it on your fridge so that you keep an eye on your eating as you reach for another glass of wine.

Everyday:
- yogurt—provides "good" bacteria for your digestive system
- two pieces of fruit
- fresh vegetables
- eight glasses of water to keep you and your skin hydrated
- a cup of green tea—a great antioxidant (keep it at work and remember to drink it)
- whole-grain bread—for fiber.

At least once a week:
- oily fish—sardines, mackerel, or salmon
- nonoily fish—cod, trout, or haddock
- unsalted nuts—pistachios or cashews

- garlic and onions
- green and yellow fruits and veggies—melon, corn, peppers, or peas
- dried fruit—apricots, pears, figs, or prunes

If you must—not very often and definitely not more than once a week:

- chocolate—make it organic, dark chocolate to feel more saintly while you're being naughty
- cake, croissants, cookies
- fizzy mineral water
- fried food
- "diet drinks"—artificial sweeteners may be a health hazard
- fast food—high in saturated fat and calories

Girly get-your-veggies-in tip
Grab a bag of precut veggies and some hummus from the supermarket, and eat when you're having a drink—it'll soak up the booze a bit and make sure you get your veggie fix at the same time.

I desperately need to lose weight, but I love grazing...

Having lots of the right snacks on hand is the number one secret. First, don't have anything in your cupboards or fridge that will blow your resolve to lose weight, and second, keep loads of healthy snacks on hand so that you're not tempted to run out to the shops for chips or some chocolate.

Keep in the cupboard:

- dried fruit is really sweet—try bananas, apricots, pears, figs, and prunes
- rice cakes, to be topped with avocado, low-fat hummus, or cream cheese
- mixed, fresh nuts
- chili olives
- pumpkin seeds

Girly supplements
Girly vices like cigarettes, alcohol, and coffee all deplete your body of Vitamin C, so get yourself an extremely good supplement if you are frequently out on the lash.

Or try this frozen girly treat:
Our favorite is so low-fat, it's unbelievable. All you need is low-fat, plain yogurt and some fruit: peaches, nectarines, and berries in the summer, bananas in the winter. Push the fruit through a sieve with a wooden spoon (the banana you can just mash up), add the fruit pulp to the yogurt, stir in, and freeze. You could even make popsicles.

Don't totally deprive yourself—promise yourself a chocolate bar or a huge cinnamon roll—but only once a week. Make it a regular day so you can look forward to it.

If you fail—Don't worry, chocolate may contain a lot of calories, but it is good for you, too. Its high levels of antioxidant flavonoids help to keep arteries from clogging. And remember, the darker the better.

Help, I keep getting UTIs! What can I do?

UTIs can be caused by an overdose of vigorous sex (hence its nickname, "honeymoonitis"), but can also be increased by the number of sexual partners and can lead to kidney infections. It is important to seek treatment for it quickly. Symptoms to watch out for are having to go to the loo very frequently—but only passing a few drops—and a burning feeling when you go.

Do:

- Drink plenty of water.

- Drink cranberry juice or take cranberry extract tablets.

- Moderate alcohol intake as much as possible. Also, try to cut down on caffeine, which dehydrates.

- Wear cotton undies, as silk or nylon will increase the likelihood of those nasty bacterial infections.

- Try to stay away from tights!

- Go to the loo as soon as possible after sex—urine works as a flush.

- Mix a teaspoon of baking soda with some water and drink it. It will make your pee alkaline and it won't burn as much.

How to cope with an abnormal pap smear result

Don't panic, it is more common than you think—one in twelve tests is abnormal. However, it is essential that you make an appointment with your doctor who will advise you of the next step—whether treatment is necessary or not. An annual pap smear is a girly must.

It is even more important to have regular pap smears if you:

* smoke.
* have a lot of sexual partners.
* lost your virginity under age twenty.

But, the most important risk factor for cervical cancer is not having a pap smear. Early detection and treatment of precancerous cells is essential.

Girly guide to the dreaded yeast infections

Few of us have avoided this irritating problem, often caused by taking too many antibiotics, which kill the good bacteria in our system. There are creams easily available over the counter, and yogurt can be used in the same way, but also:

- take acidophilus tablets or eat yogurt regularly.
- steer clear of yeast-based or fermented foods (alcohol, cheese, mushrooms, vinegar, pickles, and bread).
- avoid nylon or silk underwear and "intimate" toiletries like vaginal sprays, powders, and douches.
- a soak in a warm salt bath is soothing (add five tablespoons salt to bath).

Help I suffer from bloating and wind...

It's so embarrassing—I don't want to fart in front of my bloke!

Here's how to have near-perfect digestion

- Take a digestive supplement to help improve your system—especially important to take after you've been using antibiotics.
- Eat yogurt everyday.
- Avoid sugar and refined flour products like pasta and white bread.
- Eat more food to help your digestion, such as bananas, honey, tomatoes, leeks, asparagus, garlic, and onions.
- Chew your food properly—don't gulp.

Girly vitamin tip
Take your vitamin supplements in the morning. They may overstimulate you and keep you from sleeping if you take them at night. Then again...if you're planning a romp with your man, go for it!

Vitamins

Most of us don't always eat all the foods we need to get the right amounts of vitamins and minerals, so taking a supplement or two really does help. Not only will they decrease your chances of getting ill, but they help boost your body during times when you are run down and vulnerable. If you take nothing else, a simple multivitamin and mineral tablet with breakfast is a good start.
See p. 130 for the girly guide to boosting your immune system during the party season.

Other useful vitamin, mineral, and herbal supplements:

* evening primrose oil—for PMS
* ginseng—for energy and emotional and mental balance
* fish oils—great for menstrual cramps and will ward off osteoporosis
* zinc—if you're prone to zits or irritable bowel syndrome, or for pill users
* selenium—an antioxidant that's great for the immune system and promotes a healthy mental and emotional balance
* vitamin E—for your immune system and for skin (see p. 56)
* vitamin C—a great immune-system booster for smokers and those coming down with a cold
* vitamin B complex—great for stress and B6 aids hormonal balance

I go really wild with rage before my period— how can I keep my hormones under control?

Hormones have a huge influence on your physical, mental, and emotional well-being. It's tempting to curl up on the sofa with a chocolate bar and avoid exercise just before and during your period. Don't force yourself to go to the gym, but try to do a little gentle exercise—it will actually make you feel better. Put the TV on, throw a big cushion on the floor, and do some simple stretches. See the lazy girl's exercise tips on p. 133.

Comfort yourself

While you're on the sofa feeling sorry for yourself, nibble on some pumpkin seeds and eat a banana. Or make yourself a huge avocado and cheese sandwich. These foods will elevate your serotonin levels, which make you calmer and happier.

If you've got cramps...

Boost your endorphins—your body's natural painkiller. They help to reduce pain and give a feeling of euphoria. Jogging or aerobics will help, if you feel up to it. If you want to stay on the sofa, be sure to eat Vitamin C-rich foods like oranges, kiwi fruit, strawberries, and rose hip tea.

Can't cope, gotta have coffee and chocolate

Make your morning fix of cappucino a decaf before and during your period. If you really must have chocolate, make it a good-quality bar with a high-cocoa content and enjoy it.

Emergency teas for the cupboard

Peppermint Calms upset stomachs, indigestion, headaches, and tension. Also can be used as an emergency mouthwash.

Chamomile Relieves stress, anxiety, insomnia, and stomach trouble. Also can help UTIs.

Lemon balm Helps with anxiety, indigestion, mild depression, and irritability, and is a soothing mouthwash for an aching tooth.

Nettle Excellent for the skin—good to have on hand if you're having a few eruptions.

Green tea High in antioxidants.

Lazy girly's exercise

We never, ever exercise unless it's in front of the TV or incidental, like walking to the pub for a pint.

- Put a cushion between your knees—squeeze and hold for a count of ten, release, and repeat as many times as you can.

- An afternoon walking around the shops can also pass as exercise, if you walk fast between shops and go to a lot of shops!

- At the bus stop or subway station, always use the wasted time to do buttock clenches.

Don't eat veggies during PMS?

Yes, it's true. But don't forego all vegetables, just broccoli and brussels sprouts, which contain estrogen—a hormone you don't need more of in the days before your period.

Sometimes I worry about the effect of all that vodka and white wine...

The liver is your detox organ. It's responsible for dealing with and eliminating toxins, but we heap demands on it by drinking and eating sugary and fatty foods. If you've been boozing a lot, make your liver's job a bit easier by eating foods that are easy to digest and process.

If you don't look after your liver, you will be more prone to infections and those colds that go on for weeks and take forever to shake off.

Fruits for the liver

Stock up when you know you're going to have a heavy weekend and make a giant fruit salad using any of the following:

apricots	cranberries	papayas
avocados	grapefruit	pineapple
bananas	lemons	watermelon
berries	oranges	

> **Did you know?**
> An unbalanced liver could be the cause of mood swings, allergies, food sensitivities, fluid retention, yeast infections, and energy lows.

How to be a sensible girly and look after your health

- Check your breasts every month just after your period—your doctor can show you how. See a doctor straight away if you have any worries.

- If you think you've got any infections down below, get it checked out straight away.

- Keep up-to-date with your pap smears.

- Have a dental check-up every six months.

- Get any lumps or raised moles checked out as soon as possible.

Serious girly moment...

Sexually transmitted diseases (STDs) are on the rise. A recent report put the number of people with STDs as one in ten. If you have more than one sexual partner (lucky girl), it is especially wise to have regular checkups, as certain infections, such as chlamydia, can go unnoticed and lead to pelvic inflammatory disease, which can leave you infertile.

It's not just a girly thing
Make sure you get your partner checked out as well. It's all well and good for you to be tested and receive treatment for an STD—but not if he gives it back to you afterwards.

Above all, have fun, look after yourself, and if you can't always be good, at least take your vitamins, drink plenty of water, and eat plenty of fruits and vegetables.

Girly
Notes

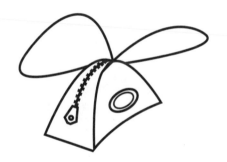

Keep those phone numbers handy...

Name   **Phone #**

Don't forget to...

1.

2.

3.

4.

5.

6.

7.

8.

9.

10.

Shopping list...

(i.e., What beauty supplies can I not live without?)

Rate your man page...

(An easy way to keep track of all your blokes.)

For your girly thoughts...
(Those bursts of genius.)